PUT THE ART IN THE ART OF WAR

Sun Tzu wrote his famous battle treatise in the sixth century B.C. for Ho Lu, King of Wu. The story goes that after reading the book, Ho Lu asked Sun Tzu if he would test his theories with a demonstration...using the 180 ladies living in the palace. When the women, divided into two companies, each with a designated leader, failed to listen to Sun Tzu's initial commands, he executed the leaders (over the king's protests, it should be noted). When they repeated the exercise, the ladies did not fail to follow Sun Tzu's commands. The king was so impressed with Sun Tzu's ability to command an "army" that he appointed him general. It turned out not to be a bad appointment, as Ho Lu's armies won major victories in the west and in the north—while Sun Tzu's fame spread.

What can we learn from his book? Though first written more than 2000 years ago, *The Art of War* wasn't translated into English until the 20th century. While translations differ, one thing they agree on is that rather than the nitty-gritty specifics about warfare, it is about *strategy and tactics*...strategy and tactics that are often now applied to business, politics, and everyday life (executions aside, of course).

Though the 13 chapters have titles such as "Waging War," "The Army on the March," and "The Use of Spies," their lessons needn't refer to the battlefield alone. Consider the lesson, "the general who loses a battle makes but few calculations beforehand." Certainly we can relate, as few us can pull off a big presentation (or even an elaborate dinner party) without adequate preparation. Or ponder this lesson: "The control of a large force is the same in principle as the control of a few men: it is merely a question of dividing up their numbers." It is perhaps obvious that delegating responsibilities at work or tasks at home—rather than doing them all yourself—is often the best approach to getting things done efficiently.

So how does all of this connect to a coloring book? The rhythm and tactile experience of applying color to paper helps you connect to your body, while the simple act of picking up a crayon or marker can calm the mind. When you're focusing on coloring a dragon or a lantern, you can quiet your everyday thoughts. Put another way, coloring is one way to exhibit mindfulness. While Sun Tzu's contemporary, Confucius, might not have taught coloring, he did teach mindfulness-based contemplative practices. These practices have since been shown to have a positive effect on executive functions such as working memory capacity, which is important in problem solving.

Too much of a stretch? Well, take heart because the best part is that coloring is accessible to everyone. Even if you lack artistic experience, you can still create beautiful, finished pieces. Having guidelines eases performance anxiety, and being able to add your own colors helps make the experience more personal. And despite whatever you have going on in your life right now, there is no right or wrong way to color in these pages.

The act of meditative coloring combined with the contemplative subject matter inspired by the oldest and best compendium of military science are meant to work together to create a powerful, creative experience. Pick a page, grab some colored pencils or gel pens, and color your way through a bit of history.

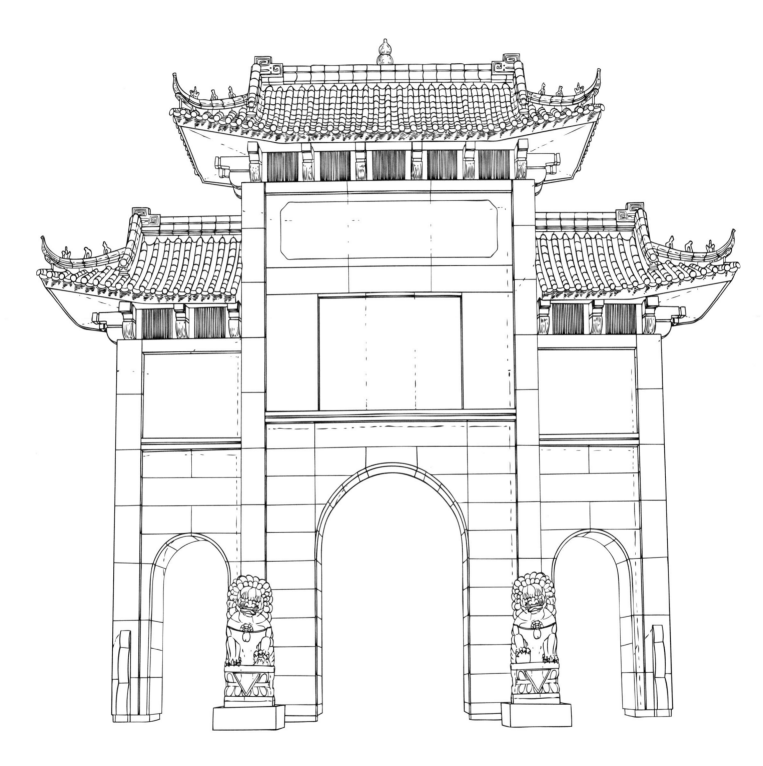

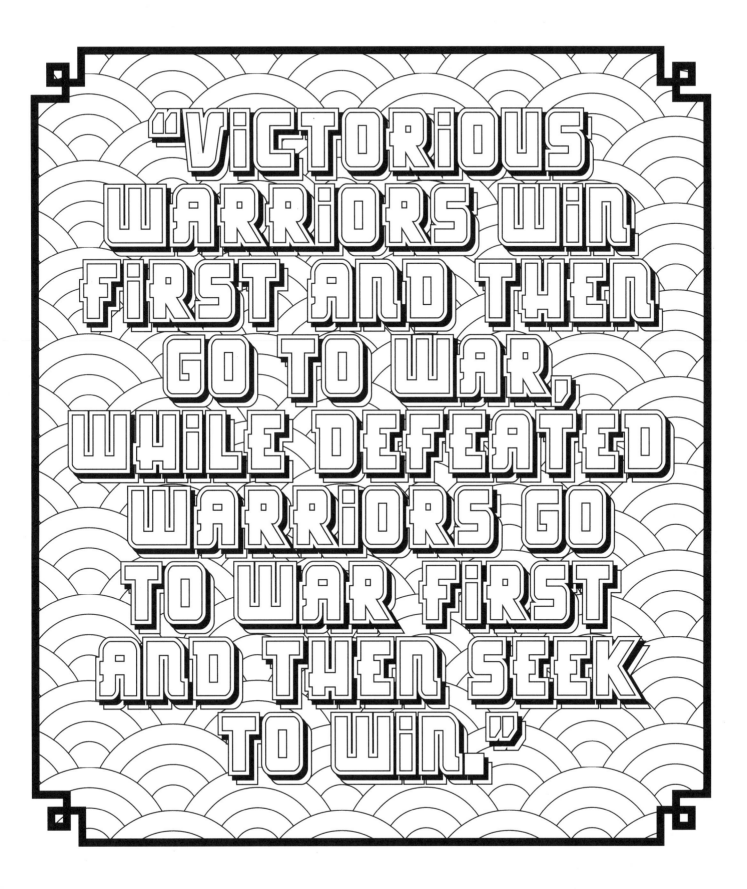

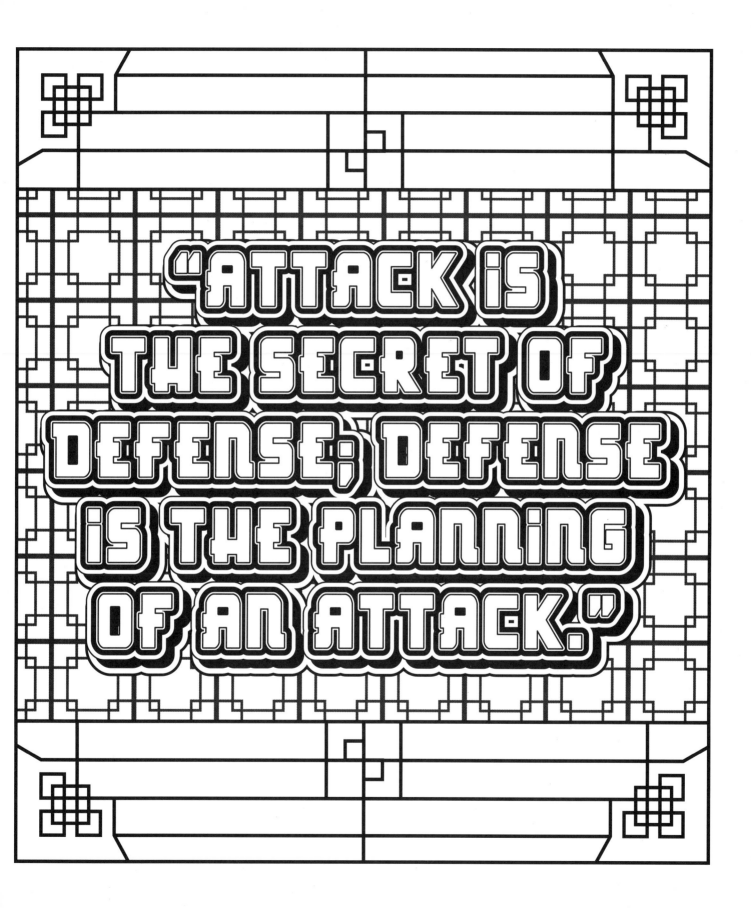

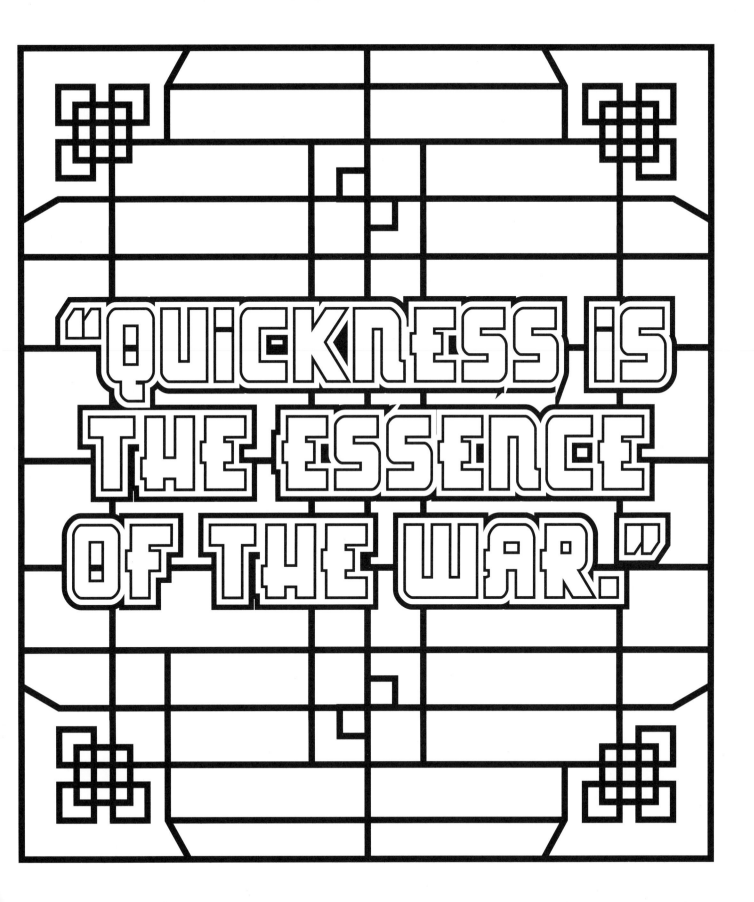

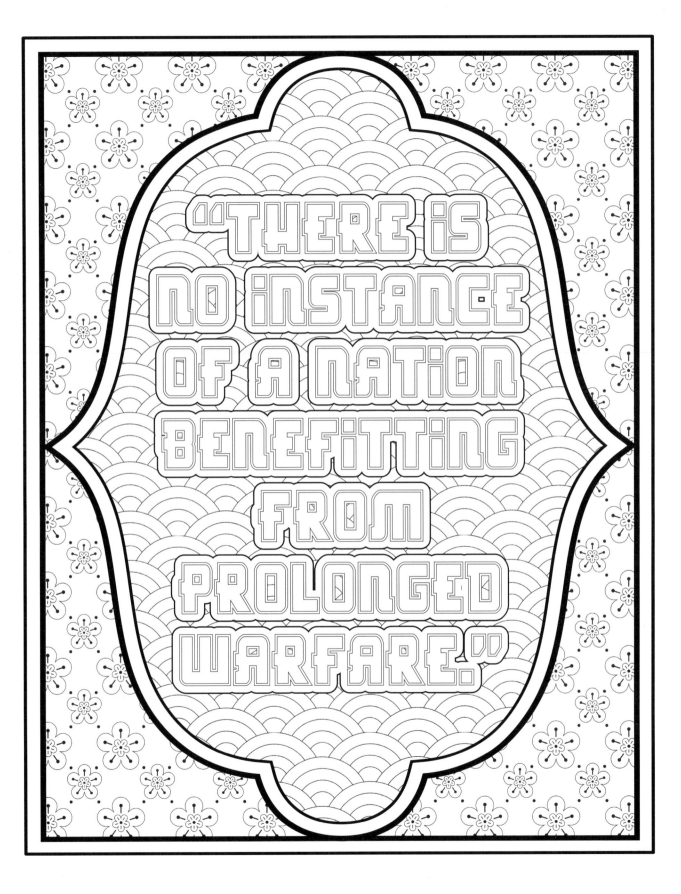

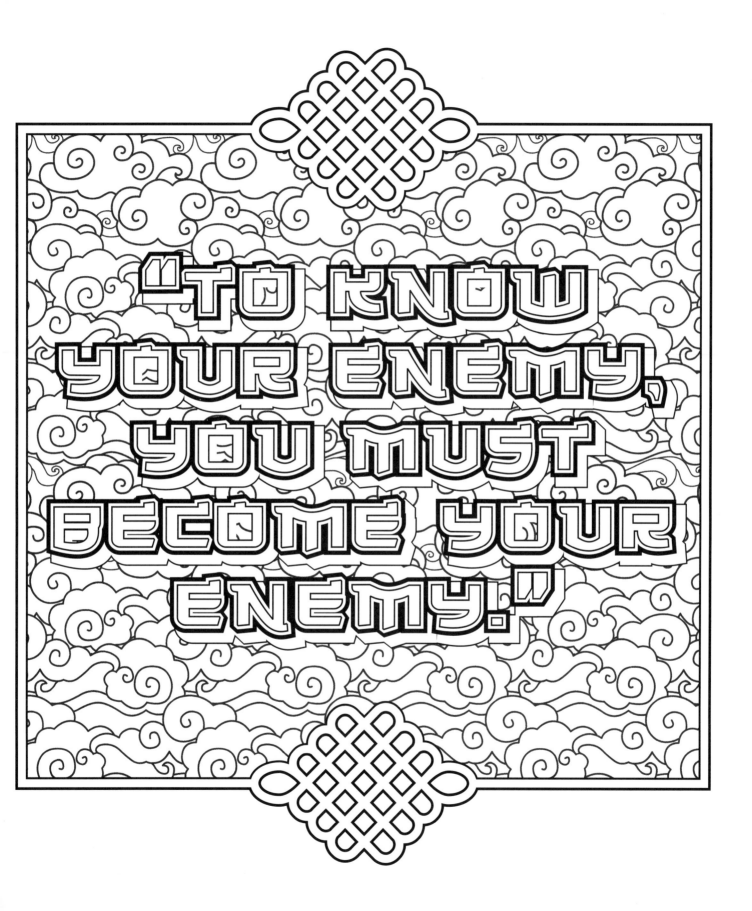

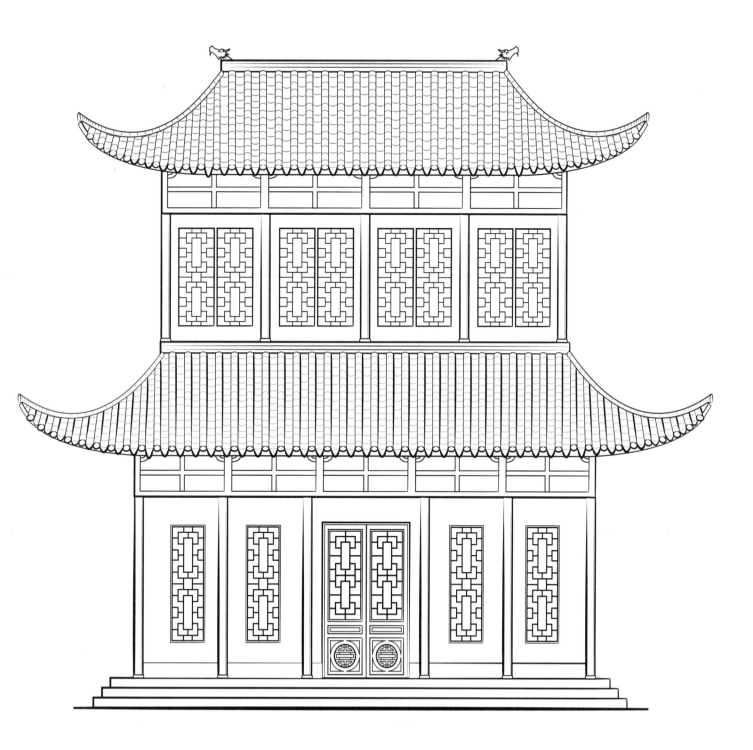

Brimming with creative inspiration, how-to projects, and useful information to enrich your everyday life, quarto.com is a favorite destination for those pursuing their interests and passions.

This edition published in 2023 by Chartwell Books,
an imprint of The Quarto Group
142 West 36th Street, 4th Floor
New York, NY 10018 USA
T (212) 779-4972 F (212) 779-6058
www.Quarto.com

10 9 8 7 6 5 4 3 2 1

Chartwell titles are also available at discount for retail, wholesale, promotional, and bulk purchase. For details, contact the Special Sales Manager by email at specialsales@quarto.com or by mail at The Quarto Group, Attn: Special Sales Manager, 100 Cummings Center Suite 265D, Beverly, MA 01915, USA.

ISBN: 978-0-7858-4254-5

Publisher: Wendy Friedman
Senior Managing Editor: Meredith Mennitt
Senior Design Manager: Michael Caputo
Designer: Sue Boylan
Editor: Jennifer Kushnier
Image credits: Shutterstock

Printed in China